CONSTITUTION 2050

CONSTITUTION 2050

RAYMUND EICH

CV-2 Books • Houston

FOREWORD

When I grew up, my family wasn't politically active, though my dad had strong opinions he frequently expressed by yelling at Walter Cronkite during the nightly news. We had a lot of books around the house, including some early 1960's civics class textbooks my parents acquired during their immigration and naturalization process. As a child, I read voraciously and put too much effort into impressing teachers and authority figures, so I read those textbooks. And learned a lot. Did you know that, under a literal interpretation, the United States Air Force is unconstitutional? (But the World War II-era US Army Air Corps wasn't). When a friend asked me how the Electoral College worked, thanks to those books, I explained it and he said for the first time he understood it.

Around the same age, I started reading Clarke, Niven, and *Analog* magazine, and my life-long interest in science fiction started. Science fiction has long been a sandbox for political speculation, going back five centuries to the proto-science-fiction of Sir Thomas More's *Utopia*. Closer to home, you can see science fiction examining political concepts in every other episode of *Star Trek*, when Captain Kirk reforms or topples corrupt and incompetent regimes with a couple of right hooks and the self-confident optimism of the New Frontier era.

Written science fiction has been set under all sorts of governments, from the UN-one-world-governments of Poul Anderson's Polesotechnic League future history and Larry Niven's Known Space series, to the Victorian throne & altar empire of Jerry Pournelle's CoDominium universe, to the anarchic socialism of Iain M. Bank's Culture series and the Trotskyite anarcho-capitalism of Ken MacLeod's *The Star Fraction* and its sequels.

Hence, early in my aspirations to write science fiction, the knowledge I could use the genre to tell stories touching on government and politics lodged in the story factory in my subconscious.

Decades passed. 9/11 happened. It was the first time foreign forces inflicted mass casualties on U.S. territory since Pearl Harbor, and it came after about a decade when respectable thinkers told Americans that history had ended and Western civilization had won. In times when a society's opinion leaders are proven horribly wrong, people don't just want information, they want a framework to make sense of that information. And the Internet, a relatively new medium at the time, gave the microphone to new thinkers and new voices. Thus, like many other people with libertarian mindsets in those months and years, every day I followed blogs like Glenn Reynolds' at www.instapundit.com.

From Reynolds' blogroll, I found other bloggers whom I read off and on in that era. One of them, perhaps Tyler Cowen at www.marginalrevolution.com, posted a blog entry asking his readers to propose new amendments to the U.S. Constitution.

Although I never posted it at the time, the Twenty-Eighth Amendment—meaning the concept behind the speculative amendment, not the story by that name you're about to read—came to my mind as a result.

Inventing other Constitutional amendments became a game my subconscious played for many years. Inspiration could pop up from anywhere. I'm not the first to propose limiting Supreme Court justices to staggered eighteen-year terms. That amendment makes sense as a way to recognize political realities that the founders didn't contemplate, much like the Twelfth Amendment recognized the ways political parties gamed the original Electoral College. Complaints made by a legal immigrant of my acquaintance about anchor babies inspired another. A third emerged in part from a factoid I heard from science fiction writer Benjamin Rosenbaum, that kosher food is halal (religiously acceptable for practicing Muslims). And the most outlandish amendment you'll read about in this book is an attempt to put into words the difficult-to-articulate feeling shared by a lot of the working-class middle Americans I grew up with, that something in Washington went very wrong, and it will take a drastic change to set it right.

But the concepts behind the amendments themselves weren't enough to generate the stories you're about to read. There's a very strong reason why nobody these days reads More's *Utopia* or any of a hundred other stories set in "perfect" societies. It's the flip side of the reason why *1984*, *Brave New World*, *The Hunger Games*, *The Handmaid's Tale*, and numerous other dystopian books remain popular.

There's never a satisfying story about when things go right. Stories are only enjoyable when they show things have gone wrong.

In stories about governments and politics, how can things go wrong? Though he wasn't an author of fiction, James Madison put his finger on two ways in *The Federalist #51*:

> In framing a government which is to be administered by
> men over men, the great difficulty lies in this: you must
> first enable the government to control the governed; and
> in the next place oblige it to control itself.

In this book, the texts of the amendments aren't the stories. When politicians try to take powers the amendments deny them, or individuals try to skirt laws the amendments authorized Congress to pass? *That's* when the stories happen.

—*Raymund Eich*
January 2020

THE TWENTY-EIGHTH AMENDMENT

1. *Each person holding an office established under Articles One, Two, or Three of this Constitution, or holding an office to which he or she is appointed by the President with the Advice and Consent of the Senate, shall at all times be subjected to the following, except as exempted in Section 2 of this article of amendment:*

A. Videography and audiography of his person and his or her utterances;

B. Recordation of his or her telecommunications to and from all other persons; and

C. Copying his or her non-electronic communications to and from all other persons;

with the products of Subsections A–C being immediately provided and archived in electronic form, to which access shall be granted without restriction to any citizen of the United States.

2. *Each person subjected to Section 1, Subsection A of this article of amendment shall be exempted therefrom under the following circumstances, provided a log of all persons whom he or she met during the period of exemption, is kept and provided under Section 1 of this article of amendment:*

A. If he or she is an Ambassador, when outside the United States, when speaking with an officer of a foreign government;

B. If he or she is the President, a Minister having authority over foreign affairs or war, or a member of Congress authorized by Law to monitor foreign affairs or war, when discussing a foreign government, after a state of war with that foreign government has been declared under Article One, Section 8 of this constitution, until such state of war has ended;

C. When alone or only with members of his or her immediate family, when at his or her residence, or at a place provided for his or her rest or recreation.

President James Archer held his umbrella with his left hand while using his right to scroll through social media messages on his smartphone. October rain plopped on the deep blue plastic, barely audible over the engines of the Marine One helicopter fleet idling on the White House lawn. The grass slapped his black leather shoes with rainwater.

He walked with a straight back, smartphone held at eye level. Have to look presidential, strong posture, for the cameraman ten feet to his right. Beads of water on the lens would give the video a somber reality. It would look good in the history videos, President Archer, resolute during an international crisis.

Next message. *@POTUS why dont you just wetwork Abdullah? Solve #KurdistanVsMesopotamianRepublicCrisis with 1 bullet?*

President Archer pressed the home button. "Tuxi," he said to the software assistant, his voice deep and rich for the parabolic mic pointed at him by the soundman, "compose a reply. '@USAFan_65706, it's illegal for me to target a foreign leader unless we declare war. Mesopotamia will comply with treaty obligations without need for war.' Post it."

The steel blue hulk topped with white of his Marine One loomed ahead. President Archer slipped his phone into an outer pocket of his overcoat. At the foot of the stairs, a Marine in dress uniform, tanned face impassive in the rain, snapped a salute. President Archer returned the salute, then trotted up the stairs.

He handed over his umbrella to the purser, said "Yes, black" to her query about coffee, and took a seat on padded beige leather at the rear of the cabin. The moment of privacy ended when the cameraman and soundman stomped into the cabin, dripping rainwater on the entry mat. The black circle of the lens and the white plastic mic dish swung instantly into position.

Back in the damn fish bowl, but he kept the thought away from his face.

At Camp David, he would have more than enough privacy.

His aides slipped past the cameraman and the soundman and took seats along the side of the cabin, half-turned toward him. Patel and McGruder strapped in. A shared glance showed they had an agenda they wanted to squeeze into the forty-five minute flight.

President Archer raised his hand until the aroma of coffee reached his nose. The purser set down the cup and saucer with a clank on the plastic flip-up table. The presidential seal on both cup and saucer faced him. Well done.

Muffled by the cabin's soundproofing, the rotors spun up, thumping the air. So too did the rotors of the other two helicopters, the decoy fleet. The purser slammed the hatch. Moments later, they rose.

Patel and McGruder peppered him with problems. Unemployment numbers up. Manufacturers rattled by the firebombing of an automated fulfillment warehouse in rural Missouri. Accusations of bribes to lower-level officials at the Energy Department to influence the solar-to-nuclear mix in the post-carbon energy plan. And updates on the Middle East crisis, a Mesopotamian riverine gunboat had fired at a Kurdistan patrol in the disputed region.

He replied to all their statements without looking at the camera, but acutely aware of it. You're a damn actor, like Nero, or Justinian's wife, one step above a prostitute. Look solemn but not somber. Speak from deep in your chest. Glance thoughtfully out the tinted windows at suburban sprawl giving way to greening fields and forests sprouted with leaves. Utter soundbites. Work in your proposed solutions, allocate more funds for job retraining, break the power of the government workers' union and grant the President the same power to hire and fire employees as any private sector CEO.

And seek peaceful solutions to the Middle East crisis—sanctions, the seizure of assets held in the US by Abdullah and other Mesopotamian Republic leaders, the hacking of Mesopotamian government computer systems.

Trees covered rolling hills. The helicopter descended toward a clearing in a thinner part of the forest. The lodges of Camp David came into view, from the outside looking like the houses of prosperous Iowa farmers he'd backslapped and glad-handed during the campaign. Wheels touched the landing pad. The rotors whirred to a stop.

The purser opened the door. President Archer ambled down the stairs, his aides two steps behind. Cloudy sky, but no rain. He could sense the camera lens and the parabolic mic aimed at his back. A Marine guard at the foot of the stairs, an African-American double of the one on the White House lawn, saluted. President Archer returned the salute, then followed a paved path leading to the right.

"Mr. President," Patel said, "we still haven't discussed the inquiry-based learning initiative—"

President Archer raised his hand, then turned. He put on his kindly, slightly exasperated uncle face, and ignored the camera and microphone behind Patel's shoulder. "We're going to meet in the main lodge—" He jerked his thumb away from his path, toward the largest of the buildings. "—tomorrow at 10, aren't we?"

"But Mr. President—"

"Melissa and the kids have been here most of the afternoon. I'm going to spend some time with my family. See you in the morning." He walked away.

A scrape of hard leather soles behind him, then the clack of Patel and McGruder following another path toward their guest quarters in the main lodge. But the sneakered feet of the cameraman and the soundman still padded on his trail.

The Secret Service personnel in their dark overcoats and sunglasses not needed under the clouds circled the private lodge. One waited on the front porch for President Archer and scowled at the cameraman and soundman trudging up the steps behind him. President Archer held the storm door open for the cameraman, then opened the main door and went in.

A fire crackled in the living room. He went to Melissa, on the couch with her denim-clad legs tucked under her. She looked up from her e-reader for one kiss. "Glad you could make it," she said.

He put on a lazy grin. "It's like the world would stop without me."

"Kurdistan and Mesopotamia can't figure it out themselves?"

"I inherited a lot of messes, and no one tells you how much work it is to clean them up. But enough about work."

She looked with offended dignity to the cameraman and the soundman. "He is off-duty, you realize."

The cameraman spoke. "We have to make sure it's just family." A minor violation of protocol.

A closer look. Sandy hair, narrow and deep-set brown eyes. A new man on the rotation.

President Archer hadn't noticed. Their lenses all looked alike.

"I'll give them the tour, Liss. And on my way I'll hug my kids. Andrew!"

His eight-year-old boy dropped his tablet on the couch and jumped up. President Archer tousled his hair and promised to take him to the outdoor basketball court in the morning if it wasn't raining. Gretchen was thirteen, hunched over her pubescent body in an armchair facing the windows, watching a teen drama on her tablet. The headphones over her blond hair bonked his forehead as he bent to kiss her. She turned him her cheek, refusing to let the camera see her face. She'd warm up soon, after the recording team gave him his 2-C time.

"Where's Hal?"

"Check the pool," Melissa said, head down at her book.

President Archer looked out the window and down. The black-helmeted head of their seventeen-year-old son bobbed above the lip of the drained pool, then descended. The whirr of skateboard wheels on gunite barely reached him through the double panes of bulletproof glass.

He turned back toward the room. For a moment, he'd forgotten the remorseless round eye of the camera, the grasping dish of the parabolic mic.

He huffed out a breath. Soon enough, he'd get them out of his life and work for the next eighteen hours. "Follow me. I'll show you it's just family."

Kitchen. Empty except for Hal's unwashed snack dishes in the sink. Media room, projection screen dark. Only the green standby light of the receiver pierced the windowless darkness. Upstairs, the kid's rooms, beds crisply made that morning by the now-absent lodge staff. In Andrew's room, plastic construction bricks spilled onto the bedspread. Closets held nothing but bare rods and empty hangers.

Back downstairs to the master suite. Windows flanked the king bed's headboard. More windows in the sidewalls gave views of the greening lawn. To the left, a Secret Service agent stood twenty yards from the lodge, his back to the window, his face to the forest. From the right came the whirr of Hal's skateboard wheels, interrupted by a clatter and the stomp of rubber soles.

Master bathroom, empty. Melissa had placed his toiletries bag near the vanity sink farthest from the window of frosted glass block. The scent of cedar paneling filled the closet. The motion sensor activated the ceiling-mounted LEDs when he entered. His casual shirts already hung from the bar on his side of the closet. In the corner nearest his shirts, the immense built-in chest of drawers, five feet high and four wide, would have neat stacks of his sweaters and his jeans. More than enough clothing for a weekend, but Melissa always overpacked, and he loved her for it.

Because the built-in's drawers were too small to hide a person, President Archer didn't lead the recording crew to it.

The camera lens swept the closet, then aimed at him again. President Archer led the way out of the closet and to the door of the master suite. For the first time, he looked the cameraman in the eye. "You agree I'm alone with my family?"

"We have videographic evidence indicating the conditions of Amendment Twenty-Eight, Section 2, Subsection C prevail." The cameraman recited the words stiffly and earnestly. Definitely new to the rotation.

The soundman, with buzzcut black hair and Korean eyes and cheekbones, rattled off his line like a bored actor. An old hand.

Joy bubbled in President Archer's gut. Sometimes the recording crew insisted on seeing the Secret Service's logs that the lodge had been swept for stowaways and no visitors had come since. Either the soundman or the training staff at the Government Transparency Office had blunted any gung-ho tendencies the new cameraman might feel.

President Archer's right hand went to the knot of his tie. "I'll be back to work at the main lodge tomorrow morning at 10. You can see yourselves out."

The cameraman and soundman stepped into the hallway. President Archer closed the door on them. Pressed the lock button. The click echoed through the room.

He stood in front of the mirror and retightened his tie. He listened for sounds from the front door.

Hinges squeaked. Sneakers thumped on the front porch. The cameraman and soundman's voices sounded on the path heading to the main lodge.

President Archer went deeper into the master bedroom. The Secret Service agent continued to watch the woods. Hal kept skateboarding.

Back to the closet. The lights blinked on. He slid shut the closet door, even though the door lay out of line of sight from the lawn and the pool. He thumbed the lock.

At the built-in, he crouched and pulled the bottom drawer all the way out and set it aside. He reached into the vacated space and groped for the button. Left side, back, high. There.

He pressed the button. A clunk sounded, the lock on the hidden hinge releasing, and the built-in chest of drawers hopped up an inch.

He stood and stooped. The built-in swung open silently on its hidden hinge. An LED puck lit up an opening in the wall almost as tall and wide as the built-in. The back wall of the opening, well within his reach, held a ladder. Stippled rubber clad the top of each wide rung in bright orange. Handrails covered with the same material ran down the sides. The ladder led down toward a brighter glow.

President Archer stepped onto the ladder.

Two steps down and he no longer had to stoop under the top of the opening. Two more steps and he came to a framed piece of paper on the back wall between rungs. The framed paper had its own tiny spotlight. He always hesitated and read the handwritten block letters.

Governing the American people is like raising small children. If you don't lie to them sometimes, you aren't doing it right.

—followed by the distinctive scrawled signature of President

Williamson, who'd advocated the Twenty-Eighth Amendment and smiled for the cameras as he signed into law the bill establishing the Government Transparency Office.

God bless you, you hypocritical bastard. President Archer grinned and kept descending.

Down, below the level of the basement full of wax-and-sawdust firelogs under the living room. His sixty-year-old knees creaked a little from effort, but adrenaline kept him going.

Finally he came to the lower basement, not present on any floor plan of the lodge. Ten feet by twelve, concrete block walls and cement floor. A dehumidifier in the corner battled dampness.

Along the far wall, the white metal grill of a floor drain lay on a rug, half under a futon configured as a sofa. On the futon sat a man in khakis and a royal blue sweater over a buttoned-down shirt of cornflower blue. His attire could place him at any one of a million desks at any one of a thousand offices in Virginia, Maryland, or the District. But when he tossed a paperback novel back on the stack and looked up, his face betrayed him. Cold eyes of greenish-blue, a solid jaw, thick eyebrow ridge. The face of a man who'd shot and stabbed long before he took up a duty station behind a desk.

The man rose. "Mr. President."

"Sit, Miller." Damned if that was his real name. Damned if President Archer even knew his agency. But the man got results.

Miller sat on the futon. President Archer pulled up a rolling chair of ergonomic shapes and black webbing. "Wetworks," he said.

Miller nodded. "Just Abdullah?"

"Yes." President Archer preempted an objection bunching up in Miller's thick eyebrows. "I know he has some hardliners who might succeed him, but it will take weeks for the Mesopotamian leadership to close ranks behind a successor."

"Your call."

"How soon?"

"By Monday morning our time. He'll have a heart attack in his mistress's bed."

"It'll look like natural causes?"

Miller blinked his greenish-blue eyes, once. "Yes."

"Make it happen." President Archer stood up.

Miller nodded and did the same. He bent down and slid the futon away from the concrete block wall, then went behind it.

President Archer couldn't see the entrance to the tunnel. Didn't even know where it led. He didn't want to.

Miller climbed down. His torso, then head, disappeared. The futon slid back into position against the wall with a rasp of wooden feet on cement. Miller's hands and thick forearms showed in the gloom under the futon, grasping for the white metal grill. Miller scraped it into position and it clattered home.

After the echoes of the metal grill faded, President Archer turned to the ladder, and climbed, toward his family, and closer to the round black lens and parabolic mic lurking beyond.

THE TWENTY-NINTH AMENDMENT

1. Any person holding an office established under Articles One, Two, or Three of this Constitution, or holding an office to which he or she is appointed by the President with the Advice and Consent of the Senate, who takes any action in word or deed contrary to the letter or the spirit of this Constitution, shall have committed the crime of contempt of the Constitution, the punishment of which shall be death.

2. A person accused of committing a crime against the person or the property of another may make an affirmative defense that the victim of that crime was guilty of contempt of the Consitution, or that the victim was attempting to protect a person that the victim knew or should have known was guilty of contempt of the Consitution.

The image of the dead girl glowed on the projection screen in Assistant U.S. Attorney Jurgensen's darkened office. Sightless blue eyes stared at nothing. The harsh morgue lights bleached her skin yet couldn't add an luster to her blond hair. The chill and gag-inducing scent of the morgue's air seemed to seep from the screen into the room, into Jurgensen's throat.

Gretchen Archer, seventeen years old, a President's daughter.

Jurgensen ripped his gaze away from the screen and reached for the bottle of antacid tablets on his paper-strewn desktop.

"Boss, you cannot seriously contemplate letting this go," Shabazz Clayton said from the other side of the desk. He stood between the two visitor chairs, fists on his hips. The other two prosecutors on Jurgensen's staff, Janice Hong and Robert Edelstein, flanked Clayton, Hong with her hands clutching the backrest of one chair, Edelstein slouching on his elbow on the backrest of the other. Hong and Edelstein nodded, more vigorously as Clayton said, "There's no doubt in the slightest that that terrorist killed her."

Jurgensen chewed and swallowed antacid tablets. Citrus flavor lingered in his mouth, a tiny dollop of pleasantness in this damned day. "You know the language of the Attempting to Protect clause of Section Two as well as I do."

Clayton rolled his lips together, then scowled at the screen. "Show the video again."

Jurgensen sighed. The video played in a background loop in his mind 24/7. It projected itself on the inside of his eyelids when he tried to sleep. He reached for his wireless keyboard and fingered the trackpad.

The morgue photo of Gretchen Archer vanished, thank Christ. The video shot by the Twenty-Eighth Amendment crew on duty that day filled the projection screen. President Archer walking through the park, approaching the podium set up near the stainless steel pillar at the northern base of the Gateway Arch. His wife, Melissa, at his side, Gretchen also next to him in a lightweight yellow sundress falling two inches below her knees. A warm spring day in the Eastern District of Missouri, in Jurgensen's jurisdiction.

Eight Secret Service personnel ringed the Presidential family. A crowd not far off-screen chanted "Contempt! Contempt! Contempt of the Constitution!" The chant lacked the glib performance of most staged protests. This one snarled. This one meant it.

Archer, to his credit, strode with a straight back to the podium. The evidence retrieved from the lodge subbasement at Camp David and the testimony of Miller, the intelligence operative, about secret meetings and illegal orders to assassinate foreign heads of state, confirmed his guilt in a quarter of a billion minds.

Next to him, Melissa gave the tight-lipped smile politician's wives learned in finishing school. Gretchen hunched her shoulders and looked down at the paved footpath.

The lead Secret Service agents broke away from the circle to flank the dais holding the podium. Jurgensen's heartburn flared for a moment. Right about now—

A disturbance in the crowd's chant. Talal Salbi pushing forward, Jurgensen knew from cellphone video sourced from the crowd. "For President Abdullah!" Salbi shouted, his English thickly accented. "For the sovereignty of Mesopatamia!"

The Secret Service agents between President Archer and the crowd melted away. Melissa Archer sidestepped, surprisingly quickly on blue designer pumps.

Gretchen looked up at Salbi with wide eyes.

The first gunshot caught President Archer in the middle of his chest. The crowd screamed, chant instantly forgotten. It's easy to call for blood but a damn sight harder to see someone spill it for you. Another shot went wide, into the space Melissa Archer had vacated.

Gretchen Archer shifted her weight forward, toward the direct line between the muzzle of Salbi's revolver and her father's chest. She turned her shoulder away from Salbi.

Trying to shield her father. So damned obvious she tried to shield her father. Even an autistic could read her intent.

Salbi's next round punched Gretchen Archer between her shoulder blade and her spine. Deep red immediately stained her yellow sundress. The autopsy later revealed the bullet clipped her aorta.

She stumbled into her father. He stumbled backward from her weight and his own gunshot wound to the heart. Father and daughter collapsed.

The camera jerked to the assassin. Salbi emptied his cylinder, rounds later recovered from a tree trunk and the dirt of the park. Those last misses didn't matter. James and Gretchen Archer were already irretrievably far along the transition from people to sacks of meat.

Jurgensen mashed the pause button on his keyboard, freezing Salbi on screen, smoking gun in his hand and a glazed smile on his face.

"She was seventeen," Hong said.

Edelstein pushed off his elbow and stood taller. "It's a PR disaster if you let this go."

"Is it?" Jurgensen said. "Seventy percent of Americans agree that Salbi should go unpunished—"

"For killing President Archer," said Clayton. "Not a seventeen-year-old girl."

"Where does the Attempting to Protect clause exempt seventeen-year-old girls?" Jurgensen said. He glared at his staff attorneys. Hong hunched her shoulders. Edelstein looked down and scratched his red-tinged brown beard.

Clayton stood stiff-backed. "The Congressional intent was that the clause applies to the Secret Service."

Jurgensen turned his glare on Clayton. "To them and everybody else."

"Congressman Evans is on the Congressional Record saying—"

"Asking whether it applies to only the Secret Service and other law enforcement personnel, and then Congresswoman Rieger gives a long-winded answer instead of expressly saying 'no.' But she meant 'no.' "

"But—"

"You're flogging a dead horse," Jurgensen said firmly. Edelstein nodded minimally. Hong winced and looked away from both her boss and her peer.

"Hey, get my back here," Clayton said sidelong to Hong and Edelstein. "Come on. You can't seriously be agreeing with boss."

Hong looked up. Her black ponytail bobbed behind her head. "The clause applies to Gretchen Archer, but she's exempt."

Jurgensen leaned back. His chair creaked. "She didn't know her father was guilty of contempt of the Constitution?"

"She was a high school junior. She didn't know politics. And she would think her father innocent of any crime."

Jurgensen massaged his forehead with stiff fingertips. "Your kids aren't teenagers yet. But the standard isn't that she knew. It's that she *should have known.*"

Hong screwed up her face. "How can you say that? A thousand websites backed by the other party have accused Archer of contempt of the Constitution since the inauguration of his first term for failing to dot an *i* and cross a *t* on some form. Gretchen wouldn't have believed her father was guilty then, why should she know he was guilty now? Kids at school? Not her parents, they would tell her her father is inno—"

"Did they?" Jurgensen said. He tapped the rewind button. The video backed away from Salbi's moment of triumph. Restored father and daughter to life. Brought the family back together. Then he pressed play.

Salbi shouted his battle cry as, off-camera, he pushed through the crowd. Then Melissa Archer stepped away from her husband. Jurgensen paused the video. "The First Lady knew he was guilty. She wasn't going to die for him."

The light of the screen glowed on Hong's cheekbones. "Even if her mother knew, she might not tell Gretchen."

Jurgensen shook his head. "You saw my email that Salbi now has that high-powered criminal defense lawyer out of L.A., Calibriani?"

"Of course I saw it. And of course I agree with you that the Mesopatamian government must be paying Salbi's legal bills. What has that got to do with Melissa Archer talking to her daughter?"

"Calibriani isn't a public defender who'll fall asleep during the trial. He knows his job. He'll put Melissa Archer on the stand."

"So?"

Jurgensen put on an oily voice. " 'Mrs. Archer, you knew your husband was guilty of contempt of the Constitution. Did you tell your children what you knew?' " His voice reverted to normal. "If she says yes, her daughter's killer goes free. If she says no, she looks like the worst mother in the world, putting her daughter into the line of fire."

"I would answer 'no'," Hong said.

"You'd commit perjury?"

Hong rocked back a half-step, then straightened her back. "To bring justice for my daughter, yes."

Edelstein let out a long sigh and shook his head.

Jurgensen nodded and said to Hong, "If it requires perjury, it can't be justice, can it?"

"Then forget justice. I'd commit perjury to avenge my daughter."

For a moment, the only sound came from the air conditioning rattling through the vents.

"Thank Christ we don't have a recording crew here," Jurgensen said. "But Melissa and Gretchen Archer had one nearby a lot."

"Not aimed at them—"

Jurgensen shook his head. "How many minutes of audio and video do we have in the public database of President Archer with his family in public or semi-public since the start of the crisis?"

Hong raised her palms. "That's on my task list for tomorrow."

"We're going to review all the footage that the facial recognition software identifies as having Melissa and Gretchen Archer in it. You know who else will? Calibriani."

"What are you getting at?"

Jurgensen used the oily voice again. " 'Mrs. Archer, you just said, under oath, that you never told your daughter that the President had committed a capital crime. You stand by that? You do. Thank you. Your Honor, I'd like to enter defense exhibit number' followed by the best video he can find of Gretchen asking her father if he was guilty and both President and Mrs. Archer trying to ignore the elephant in the room. Then Calibriani will ask if Mrs. Archer had a conversation with her daughter off-camera in which she told Gretchen of her father's guilt."

"Melissa Archer will stick to her story."

"In other words, she'll keep committing perjury?"

"She's a strong woman," Hong said. "She'll do the best she can to avenge her daughter."

Jurgensen folded his arms across his chest. He leaned back in his chair, playing it like a violin to get an ominous creak. "If our case requires the best witness to lie under oath, we don't have a case. We have a perversion of justice. And a risk of getting disbarred if the truth comes out."

Hong bowed her head and angled her shoulders away from her peers.

On the other side, Edelstein said, "You worry too much, boss."

"About losing my career?"

"None of us are going to get disbarred." Edelstein spoke with the easy cynicism of a man in his late 20s. "Even if Melissa Archer lied under oath, hell, even if we expected before she took the stand that she would lie under oath, that's a gray enough area of legal ethics. Especially because a lot of powerful people would lean on the bar association to give us a pass."

"And how do you know that?"

"I know you got a call from someone pretty high up at the Justice Department."

Jurgensen cracked his knuckles. "You lurk in the hall outside my office a lot?"

With a lazy smile, Edelstein said, "I happened to be passing by when your door was open."

Clayton and Hong shifted their weight. Both avoided Jurgensen's gaze.

"I see Edelstein told you what he heard."

"He told us something," Clayton said. "We don't know everything."

Jurgensen considered. "You guys are loyal. I'll tell you the whole story. I got a call from an assistant undersecretary at DoJ, a lady named Pulaski. She's as high up as you can get in DC without having a Twenty-Eighth Amendment recording crew following you to the bathroom door. Let me tell you, she knew how to communicate her meaning without putting it into words."

"What was her meaning?" Hong asked.

"Everyone in DC wants Salbi to get the death penalty for killing Gretchen Archer. Even everyone in the other party."

"Why would they side with President Archer?" asked Clayton.

Edelstein piped up. "Because they commit contempt of the Constitution too. As much as they can get away with." He grinned like he'd revealed some shocking truth. "If Salbi gets convicted for killing Gretchen Archer, every day on Capitol Hill will become take your daughter to work day. Or your mistress posing as your daughter."

Jurgensen said, "So Pulaski, the DoJ lady, played her carrots and her sticks. Prosecuting Salbi would put me on the short list for nomination as a full U.S. Attorney regardless who wins next year's Presidential election. Convicting him puts me at the top of the list."

He shut his eyes in a long blink. No images of Gretchen Archer on the morgue slab, or President and daughter bleeding to death under the Gateway Arch, popped up on the inside of his eyelids. Instead he saw a corner office, appearances as a pundit on the news shows, signing books, retiring by 60 to finally take that river cruise with his wife down the Danube.

He opened his eyes just before Edelstein asked, "And the sticks?"

Jurgensen forced nonchalance into his voice. "The usual. Budget cuts—"

Hong's eyes widened. "Would you have to reduce staff positions?"

He scrunched up his mouth. The antacid bottle on his desk called to him, like cheap liquor to a drunk. He met her gaze. "I would expect to have to let one of you go and overwork the other two."

Hong gasped. Clayton palmed the fade cut close to his scalp and slowly shook his head.

Edelstein, in contrast, gave a lazy grin. "Seems like an obvious choice."

"I make my life easier by wasting taxpayer money and committing my own little bit of contempt of the Constitution?"

Edelstein remained unflappable. "We're too low on the totem pole to commit contempt of the Constitution, boss. And if we don't spend our budget on this case we'll spend it on something else. And it's not just your life that gets made easier. It's ours too."

"If I get a full U.S. attorney position, one of you takes my place here?" Jurgensen creaked his chair again.

A shrug, then Edelstein said, "Or we become partners in the newly-renamed criminal defense firm of Calibriani and Clayton. Or we get book deals. Or my mom stops nagging me with how much more money and how many more children my corporate law brother has. Prosecuting Salbi for killing Gretchen Archer helps all of us, boss."

"Except if I'm at a Senate committee meeting to get confirmed as a U.S. Attorney, and some Senator asks me if my prosecution of Salbi was politically motivated. If my nomination is part of a quid pro quo."

"If it comes to that," Edelstein said, "just pick your words carefully."

"You mean, lie?"

Edelstein's lazy grin flickered, then died inside his beard.

That boy was too young and cynical… but he had a point. Senate hearings were all for show, anyway. The chairman lined up the votes before the nominee sat at the witness table. So easy. Taking that river cruise when you're young enough to enjoy it.

Jurgensen reached for the antacid bottle. He opened it and shook a tablet into his palm without looking. His gaze landed on the projection screen. The paused frame showed President Archer a fraction of a second before Salbi's bullet pierced his heart. At his side, his daughter looked up, off-camera, blond hair frozen after getting whipped up by the turn of her head. Her blue eyes showed fear, and love for her father. And a tinge of uncertainty.

She knew he was guilty of contempt of the Constitution.

She knew, but in that moment, she acted without thinking. That love for her father was real, and unlike her mother's, in earnest. And two seconds later, that love would put her in the path of a bullet.

The world needed more of that earnest love.

Jurgensen's jaws mashed the antacid tablet into orange-flavored powder. He needed something earnest too. Something more than a fast-track to promotion, and a chance to retire a few years early.

He needed to work for justice, however distasteful, however harmful to his bottom line, it might be.

Jurgensen tossed the antacid bottle onto his desk, then fixed his gaze on his staff attorneys. "We're not prosecuting anyone for Gretchen Archer's killing."

THE THIRTIETH AMENDMENT

1. The first sentence of the first Section of the Fourteenth Amendment is hereby repealed and replaced with the following:

Any person born in the United States to parents who are both citizens or permanent legal residents of the United States and are subject to the jurisdiction thereof, or any person naturalized in the United States, is a citizen of the United States and of the State wherein he or she resides.

2. Any person under the age of eighteen years who is now living, who was born to at least one parent who was neither a citizen nor a permanent legal resident of the United States, and who was considered a citizen of the United States under the first sentence of the first Section of the Fourteenth Amendment as of the date of ratification of this Amendment, shall have the right to live and work in the United States, upon attaining the age of eighteen years and demonstrating fluency in the English language.

———————————

Gonzalo's stomach flopped like a beached fish gasping for breath. The waiting room was a plain place of vinyl tile, paneling the color of caramel, and hard, misshapen plastic chairs. The only sounds came from the shifting bodies of the other twenty-two test takers and the rustle of traffic on the twelve-lane freeway a kilometer away. The United States flag hung on a pole at the front of the room, next to a picture of President Benchley, as stern as an angry saint.

Gonzalo glanced around the room. Here he was in Los Angeles, just two hundred kilometers from Mexico, but only three other test-takers looked Latin American, let alone Mexican. Four looked like Arabs—in the corner, two *negros* with brown-black skin—there were even two *rubios*, brother and sister, perhaps, blond hair and blue eyes set in wide faces. But the greatest number were *chinos*. What word did the *americanos* use? Orientals? Asians?

One *chino*, black hair spiked over a face dominated by thick-rimmed eyeglasses, spoke to the *rubio* brother. "My father, big man in party, send my mother to luxury birth hospital, Orange County."

"*Da*," said the *rubio*, then muttered something in a foreign language.

"My father bring in test prep tutor. From U.S. Spend top dollar." The *chino* smelled of cologne and cigarettes. "I ready."

Gonzalo's stomach turned more sour. Test prep tutor? He couldn't compete with that. All he'd done to learn English was press the *CC* button on television shows from San Diego. And check out books from the *americano* missionary library on Avenida Benito Juarez, books with pictures about FIFA World Cups and auto repair.

He took a breath. He didn't compete against the *chino*. It only mattered how many questions he answered right.

He glanced around again. His gaze met that of the one Latina in the room. Clear skin and black hair shiny under the fluorescent lights in the ceiling. Beautiful, but who was he to say she was too beautiful for him? He gave her a confident look. Her gaze lingered on his for a long moment, then coyly turned away.

After he started his own auto repair shop, he'd scrub the grease from under his fingernails and find her.

A door opened next to the picture of President Benchley. Everyone in the waiting room looked up. In came a tall *gringo* with stooped shoulders and a stubbly brown beard. "It's almost time to enter the testing room. Follow me."

Gonzalo and the others formed a single file and passed the *gringo* into the next room. Three rows of lockers covered the far wall. Keys with orange handles and elastic coils hung from each lock. A short *negra*—no, the *americano* missionaries, *gringo* boys in white shirts and black neckties, had told him never to call them by the Spanish words, he should instead always say *African-American*—stood with fists on her wide hips and gave orders. "Phones, smart watches, papers, books, pens, pencils, backpacks, purses, wallets, anything else you got, you put it in a locker. You get it back after the test. I'm going to say it again, phones, smart watches, anything you can use to send a message in or out, anything you might have something written down on, you cannot bring it in the test room. The only exception is that sealed packet you got from the U.S. embassy or consulate in your home country. Everything else goes in a locker."

The file broke up into a mass of people scrambling for the lockers. Gonzalo followed the Latina, but the *chino* stinking of cigarettes got in his way. Gonzalo found a locker at the end, turned the key, opened the door. He placed his wallet and his touchscreen phone inside. They looked tiny in the moment before he shut the door.

"Next," said the African-American woman, with a flick of her head to toss her long straight hair, "you're going to hand over your sealed packet and we're going to prick your finger for DNA. It ain't going to hurt. We got to do this to match you with who the packet says you are. Alright, line on up."

From the back of the line, Gonzalo craned his head. The African-American woman sat at a table near another door. With her at the table was a *china* in blue scrubs and black hair tied up in a bun. She wore rubber gloves and racks of medical supplies rested on the table in front of her.

The line crept forward, but fairly quickly. When Gonzalo's turn came, he handed the packet to the African-American woman. The *china* in blue scrubs swabbed his left index finger's tip with a cooling wipe, then squeezed his finger with one hand. He barely felt the pin prick. The *china* touched one end of a slender, two-centimeter long glass straw to the drop of blood. When blood filled the glass straw, she dropped it into a plastic tube, snapped the tube's lid closed, and sealed the lid with a sticker bearing a bar code and his name. A matching sticker resealed his packet.

They worked hard to prevent anyone from cheating.

"Go on in," the African-American woman said. She gestured at the door to the next room. Two men stood to the sides of the door. *Gringos* with buzzcut hair and bulky black vests with the ICE logo on the breast.

Gonzalo bristled—his first memory was of men like them, ordering his mother and him onto a bus bound for Tijuana—but they didn't even notice. Who were they to—

He took another breath. Nothing he could do about that now. Except pass the test.

The testing room held four rows of six chairs with flipped-open desks. Plastic-wrapped wires tied each chair to the floor, and cords tied to each chair a tablet computer in a rubberized case resting on each desk. Only two desks were empty. The distant freeway sounded much quieter. The stooped, bearded *gringo* stood near the door with a different tablet in his hand. "Name?" he asked.

Gonzalo gave his. Why did he have to? He must be the last one on the list.

The *gringo* checked the tablet. "You're on the list. Sit there." He pointed at a chair in the third row, second from the right. Next to the *chino* with spiked hair and thick-rimmed glasses.

"I have to?"

"Seats are randomly assigned with a constraint to minimize proximity of people speaking the same native language."

Gonzalo understood a few of the *gringo*'s words. "Assigned. Okay." He went to his seat. The Latina sat on the front row, on the far side of the room, her head bowed over folded hands.

Gonzalo sat. The *chino* lounged back, tablet with dark screen in his right hand. The *chino* shook his wristwatch past the end of his left sleeve. A thick mass of dials wheeled around, and a small diamond glittered in place of the number 12.

He's not your problem. The test is.

The door closed. The bearded *gringo* stayed there and the short, wide African-American woman went to the front of the room. She gave instructions about the multiple-choice test, the tablets, they had one hour, no leaving the room. Gonzalo listened carefully.

Madre de Dios, he prayed, *help me pass the test.*

"Alright everybody," said the African-American woman. "Begin."

Gonzalo's tablet screen lit up. He pressed *Start*.

The hole in his stomach enlarged. He read and reread the first question.

Incarceration is to penitentiary as:
a. Intoxication is to intermediary.
b. Admission is to hospital.
c. Departure is to garage.
d. Graduation is to university.

How the hell was he supposed to know all these complicated words? Why couldn't they do this test by speaking? The hole in his stomach sent hot tendrils up his chest. His chance to work in the U.S. was about to collapse.

Gonzalo pressed *a* and shook his head. A glance to the right showed the *chino* staring intently at the screen. His left elbow rested on the desk and he pressed the fingers of his left hand against his forehead. The *chino* entered an answer and kept going.

Gonzalo turned his attention back to his tablet. Question two. Reading comprehension. A passage from one of the *americano* documents, the Constitution or the Declaration. The hot tendrils faded, replaced by something worse, a chill fluid sensation trickling down his throat. He turned dull eyes to the first question.

According to the signers, what sort of rights are Life, Liberty, and the pursuit of Happiness?
a. Rights that only citizens, and not foreigners, have.
b. Rights that only human beings, and not alien life forms, have.
c. Rights that people can give up in exchange for other rights.
d. Rights that cannot be taken from people.

Gonzalo skimmed the passage again. *Unalienable* might mean not for aliens. But why would the *americano* founders talk about aliens?

Wait, they called *illegales* 'aliens' too. He answered *a* and pressed *next page*.

Three faint buzzes sounded somewhere to his right.

He glanced at the *chino*. A later page of reading comprehension questions. Damn, the *chino* was quick. The private tutor must have been good.

On the first question, the *chino* answered *c*.

Two faint buzzes. Did an insect fly around the room?

The *chino* answered the next question *b*. Then he cast a scowl at Gonzalo.

Gonzalo looked away just as four faint buzzes sounded. They confirmed his guess. They came from the *chino*'s wristwatch. And it looked like the *chino* answered the next question *d*.

The *chino* scowled in Gonzalo's direction. He took his left hand away from his forehead and moved it under the desk. He clamped his lower thighs together on the wristwatch.

How did the *chino* cheat? Maybe his glasses held a tiny camera and a transmitter. His 'private tutor' must wait nearby, read the question, and give him the answers by sending buzzes to the wristwatch.

Gonzalo sighed. Some people had the money and the connections to bend the rules. He didn't. So he wouldn't pass the test. Might as well put the tablet down and take a nap before his bus ride back to Tijuana.

Something solidified in his spine. Hell no. That's how Mexicans thought. They handed the steering wheels of their lives to fate and ended up going nowhere. But a piece of paper from the Los Angeles County Vital Records Office and more paper stamped by a consular clerk in Tijuana said he was an *American. Madre de Dios*, he would act like one. Maybe he would lose, like the GIs in some late night movie who were bloodied by Rommel at Kasserine, but he would fight.

He tapped *next page*.

As if in response to his new resolve, the questions got easier. One reading question rephrased a road sign as *a driver will pay twice as much for a speeding ticket*. When applying for a loan to buy a house, he reasonably guessed that the *M* in the acronym *ARM* stood for *mortgage*. He used the knowledge stolen from the *chino* to answer all the multi-question reading comprehension passages with, in order, *c, b,* and *d*.

Even after the *chino* finished early and leaned back in his chair, arms folded over his chest, right arm over left to obscure his wristwatch, Gonzalo kept battling. A miser was someone who was unhappy, right? And an author was someone who had authority? Even though doubts came in, he remembered another late-night movie, where young *gringos* and *negros* bonded on a practice field for American football. A coach yelled "play to the whistle."

Gonzalo mashed the *next page* button. Another page of reading comprehension questions, but only two of them. He couldn't use the answers taken from the *chino*. He'd have to read the whole thing.

The North Atlantic Treaty Organization (NATO)—

The screen instantly went dark.

"Alright everybody. If you haven't figured it out by now, the testing session is over." The African-American woman raised her eyebrow. If you hadn't figured it out by now, she must think you were very stupid. "The tablet will soon give you your results. If it says you failed, you will leave the room and have 72 hours to return to your countries of residence. If you fail, it isn't the end of the world, you can apply again in three years."

Someone on the front row mumbled a question. The African-American lady answered, loudly, "If you pass, you wait right here while we discharge the others."

Color flashed on all the desks. Gonzalo looked down like everyone else.

His tablet showed a red screen. Under the ICE logo appeared the stark white word *Failed*.

Gonzalo's shoulders fell. Three years before he could try again. Three years behind concrete walls topped with embedded broken bottles, on streets rendered dangerous by dueling *narcos*, working in the auto repair shop for low wages under the harsh shouts of the *jefé*.

The stink of cologne and cigarettes mauled his nose. "You fail," said the *chino*. The tablet on his desk glowed green, read *Passed*. "Too bad. You no be my lawn guy. Ha ha."

Gonzalo's cheeks burned. He turned away from the *chino*. The pressure of seventeen others leaving the room pulled him up and out of the desk. He joined the line of those who'd failed, and trudged toward the exit. Six places ahead of him, the Latina shuffled along, black hair still glossy as it slumped down the sides of her downturned face.

He came to the table just outside the door. Lockers slammed on the other side of the room. The bearded *gringo* asked for his name and found his sealed packet in a basket. The *gringo* opened the packet. A moment later he handed over Gonzalo's birth certificate. "Yours to keep," he said.

Gonzalo took it. Thick paper and English words that seemed empty of meaning. The *americanos* took such stock in such things. Rule of law. Fair play. Naive fools.

Naive fools who won world wars and invented the automobiles he worked on every day.

And thanks to the piece of paper in his hand, he was one of them.

"The *chino* next to me cheated."

The *gringo* looked up. His Adam's apple bobbed in his forward-leaning neck. "Say again?"

"The *chino*—in English should I say Oriental or Chinaman?"

" 'Asian.' " The *gringo* reached for a tablet. "What makes you think he cheated?" he asked, while he looked down at a seating chart.

"I heard his wristwatch buzz. Once it buzzed four times, bzz bzz bzz bzz, and he answered *d*. Another time, it buzzed twice, bzz bzz, and he answered *b*. A third time—" Gonzalo broke off. The bearded man's eyes looked like he'd heard enough.

But he had to believe him! "And when he noticed I could tell he was up to something, he put his left hand between his legs, where he could feel the buzz and I couldn't hear it."

The *gringo* raised his left hand. "I'm sure you saw and heard that. And his glasses had thick rims. It might be possible to hide a camera and a transmitter in them."

"So you'll fail him? Make him come back in three years?"

"If he cheated, he's barred from trying again for life. Thank you for bringing the possibility of cheating to our attention. It's very civic-minded of you. Good luck to you when you try again—"

"Possibility?" Gonzalo said. "Aren't you going to investigate?"

"I assure you, we will. If we need to."

Gonzalo rocked back on his heels. *This* was the *americano* rule of law? To favor *a*, an Asian who cheated over a Mexican who told the truth? "Need to?" he shouted.

A smile distorted the *gringo's* beard. "The second part of the exam is a test of verbal fluency."

"What does that mean?"

The *gringo* raised his palm. "We just tested how well you read and write English. The next test is how well you *speak* it."

Gonzalo's breath caught. He bowed his head, apologizing in his own mind for shouting. "I understand, sir."

"Again, good luck next time."

"Thank you," Gonzalo said, already turning away. The Latina with the long glossy hair stood at an open locker. Her trembling hand gripped the edge of the locker door. She squeezed shut her eyes, trying to close the valve of tears.

Gonzalo lifted his shoulders and went toward her. In three years, perhaps they would try again together.

THE THIRTY-FIRST AMENDMENT

The First Amendment to this Constitution is hereby modified, as follows:

Congress may make any law for the United States, and the Legislature of each of the several States may make any law for that State, regulating, restricting, or prohibiting the practice of any religion other than the Christian or Jewish religions.

Pockmarked ceiling tiles interspersed with buzzing fluorescent lights seemed poised to fall on Irving Blaustein's head. His sneakers squeaked on scuffed vinyl. The air conditioning labored to clear the stink of bad coffee and human sweat, and fell short. The greatest country on Earth and its FBI offices were cramped and dingy.

All the aches and pains of middle age suddenly turned up a notch. Maybe it wasn't the greatest country on Earth anymore.

His head drooped.

Or maybe his son was a schlemiel.

The clack of the soles of the attorney's black leather oxfords slowed. "In here," the attorney said in a brash voice. Jordan Shapiro, one of the best criminal defense lawyers in the city. But even though they went to the same temple, Shapiro wouldn't cut Irving a deal on his hourly rate.

The things we do for our children.

Shapiro opened the door. Irving had seen the room a hundred times on TV. More scuffed tile under a drop ceiling with brown splotches of leaking water, plain wood table and chairs battered from use, and a giant window into the next room.

Irving ignored the two men who rose from the table as they entered. He went to the giant window. Past smudges of fingertip oils and dirt on the other side of the glass, Phillip sat in a chair like the ones in this room, turned away from the same sort of table. Phillip folded his arms over his chest and glowered at the cross-work of bars across the single window.

Uh-oh. Irving knew that look. Phillip knew he'd broken the rules, but in his mind it was the rules' fault, not his. Four hours in FBI custody had not been enough to make him think otherwise.

Jordan Shapiro spoke with casual insistence to the two men. "I'm not going to speak with my client in the interrogation room."

One FBI agent, two inches taller than Irving and fair of skin and hair, obvious the leader, rolled eyes as blue as his suit. "You know we can't record your conversation."

"No, it's inadmissible in court. But you might record things—"

"That would be fruit of a poison tree. You know that's also inadmiss—"

"You're good at telling me what you want me to think I know. But I've seen you guys launder otherwise inadmissible evidence the way the Mafia launders money. Find us another room."

The lead agent rolled his blue eyes one more time, then turned to the second FBI man. This one was shorter than Irving, with thinning black hair on his head and wisps of more peeking above the collar of his shirt and the knot of his necktie. From his skin tone and facial features, the shorter FBI man could have a background from anywhere in a circle bounded by Tel Aviv and Tehran.

Irving suddenly hated him. He could have been the one who entrapped Phillip.

"Right on it, Landry," the shorter FBI man said, and headed for the door.

The tall one, Landry, nodded. "You two wait here."

Irving turned his palms toward the water-stained ceiling. "Can't I talk with my son?"

"Your lawyer doesn't want you to. Ghavamian will be back soon."

Landry turned away from Irving and the lawyer. He stood with his left palm flat on the table and used his right hand to turn on a tablet. One swipe later, he glanced over his shoulder at Shapiro, then lifted the tablet and carried it to a corner of the room, under a wall-mounted camera and foam-capped microphone, where he could use the tablet without being seen.

Was he writing a report? What foolish things had Phillip said before wising up enough to ask for a lawyer?

A sickly warmth came to the underside of Irving's tongue. He tapped the bottle of nitroglycerin tablets in his jacket's inner pocket. G-d willing he wouldn't have another angina attack.

He looked through the window, as if it could be the last time he saw his son. Phillip still stiff-necked. Irving could barely endure it—

The short FBI agent, the one with nothing better to do than trap a poor schmuck in a 9/11 Memorial Act violation, came back and led Irving and Shapiro away. A tiny conference room, where four rolling chairs with yellow foam peering out from tears in black plastic crowded around a circular table. No camera or microphone mounted on the off-white wallboard.

No sight of Phillip, not even through a dirty window into an interrogation chamber.

Irving's head swam. He could barely endure not seeing his son, too.

Knuckles rapped twice. Shapiro said "Come in" as the door swung open.

"Hey, you can't barge into a room where an attorney is with his client," Shapiro said to Ghavamian, but Irving didn't care. Phillip walked in, his ankles and his wrists unchained. Free enough. For now.

The door rattled shut. Irving's voice came out sharper than he'd intended. "What the hell did you do?"

"Dad, I served somebody I thought was a customer, that's all I did." The same tone of voice Phillip had used at age fourteen, claiming that he'd been searching the internet for recipes for creampie and didn't know it would bring up dirty photos.

"I leave you alone to run the shop for two hours—"

"Oh yeah, how was your JMatureKaffeeklatsch.com date?"

"This is no time for jokes!" Irving said. Then his fire burned down. He pulled out a rolling chair and slumped onto his elbows on the table.

"You look familiar," Phillip said.

"Jordan Shapiro. You've probably seen me around Beth Yeshurun. I'm your lawyer."

"I haven't hired you."

Shapiro enunciated each word. "Your father is paying my bills. Because he's trying to save your skinny ass from five years in a Federal prison."

"They can't give me five years for this. Can they?"

"You've heard of the 9/11 Memorial Act, haven't you?"

"Of course I have. But outlawing the practice of Islam in the United States? it's unconstitutional."

"Two-thirds of Congress and thirty-eight state legislatures say otherwise."

"Un-American, then."

Shapiro stared at him, then rolled his wrist and extended his hand like a fighter plane attacking one of the empty chairs. "Sit, and tell me what happened, before you give your father another angina attack."

Phillip sat, opposite Irving. Still he acted like he didn't belong here. Five years in Federal prison! If Lillian were still alive, the risk their son faced and his casual attitude toward it would break her heart. She'd never let Irving hear the end of it.

Shapiro pulled out a chair, then a phone from an inner pocket of his jacket. "This will record and transcribe our conversation." He set the phone on the table and pressed the red button on the touchscreen. "Interview with client Phillip Blaustein. Tell me what happened."

"I was manning the shop while my dad was out. It's his usual day for errands—"

"By 'the shop' you mean Blaustein's Kosher Meat Market, on Beechnut near the freeway?"

"Yes." Phillip went on with his story. "Around one-thirty, a customer comes in. He doesn't look familiar and he's acting kind of nervous. He looks in the case and asks if all the meat is kosher. I say yes. He asks how can he know I'm telling the truth and I point to the certifications we have up on the wall behind the case and the cash register. He then asks how can he know those are real and I ask him if he wants to buy some meat or not. He then asks if kosher meat is halal—acceptable for consumption by Muslims—and I say I've heard that it is. Then he pulls out his FBI badge and puts me under arrest." Phillip held out his hands as if he couldn't understand why G-d would allow such a travesty of justice.

Shapiro shook his head of thick black curls. "You're a terrible liar."

Irving looked up. "How can you say…" he said to Shapiro, then turned to his son. Phillip sat with his arms folded over his chest and a smug grin on his face. "I should let you have a public defender who'll sleep through your trial. Maybe in five years I can remarry and get a stepson who wants to go into small business."

"The FBI agent wore a mic and a bodycam," Shapiro said. Phillip's smug grin finally faded. "If I know what he recorded, I can defend you better from how they'll use that evidence. Start over."

Phillip's eyes flicked down to the recorder. "Can they find out what I'm about to say?"

"It's attorney-client privileged. They can only find out if we tell them."

His eyes darted around the room. "They might have hidden bugs—"

"Anything they record right now is inadmissible. They know the rules and most of the time they play fair. Especially if they're fishing for a big target, they don't want to screw it up on a technicality."

Pain tightened in Irving's chest. He dug the bottle of nitroglycerin tablets from his jacket. Sweat dabbed his forehead and the back of his neck. His fingers fumbled with the child-proof cap.

"Dad, are you okay?"

"An—angina." Fishing for a big target? What had Phillip done?

Yes, Irving had sold kosher meat to people who didn't look or act Jewish, and he knew Muslims could eat kosher food, but Jews were supposed to be a light unto the nations, and a Gentile's money looked the same as a Jew's when it was all bundled up in the bank's thick blue deposit bag. But even continuing to make the sale when a customer implied he was Muslim shouldn't have been enough for the FBI to complete the sting.

The tightness pulsed in his chest. Irving lined up the tabs and pushed the cap up. What had Phillip done? Irving shook out a tablet. On how many of his errand days?

Irving rested the nitroglycerin tablet under his tongue. The tightness in his chest eased within moments. He took a breath and raised his hand. Feeling weak, but alive. "Tell us the truth."

Phillip looked down and away from his father. Irving read his expression. Finally he felt fear and guilt.

"I've been going to American Muslim sites on the Internet to drum up business."

For a moment, Irving felt the angina trying to regroup and counterattack. But the nitroglycerin tablet dissolving in his mouth kept it at bay.

"Details," Shapiro said.

"Right after the 9/11 Memorial Act passed, I knew it would be like when Ferdinand and Isabella—" His mouth twisted like he wanted to spit. "—told all the Jews and Muslims to convert or get out of Spain. A lot of our people and a lot of the Muslims pretended to convert but practiced their faiths in secret. I figured the Muslims would use the Internet to help share information on how to do so. And I remembered my friend Ben, at the Rosenbaum School, explained set theory to me in math class by saying that kosher food was halal for Muslims, but that didn't mean halal food was kosher for us."

"You went on the dark web to make business for us? Did you give away my Social Security number? Did you offer to take bitcoins in payment?" Irving's face paled. "Did you tell every Muslim in the city to come to Blaustein's? Why not put up a sign with a giant arrow pointing at the store saying *FBI, Raid Us*?"

"I was more careful than that. I called up the receptionist at the kosher butchers' trade association office in New York and sweet-talked her for the member directory. I posted the whole directory. I knew you're usually out of the shop this day of the week, so I added a note to our entry that customers should come to our shop today." His hands made small, aimless gestures in the air above the table. "But since that would be a tip to the FBI, I added similar notes to all the other entries."

Fear jolted through Irving, but the nitroglycerin kept it from squeezing his chest. "You emailed every kosher butcher in the country and asked if they want to violate the Constitution with you?"

"No, not like that. I just picked random days Sunday through Thursday."

Shapiro said, "No one else knew you were doing this?"

"It was all me. I didn't tell my dad, my friends, or anyone in the trade." He shook his head and wiped his hand side-to-side through the air.

"How did you communicate the directory to Muslims secretly practicing their religion?"

"I went on the Internet. Anonymously. I got a thumbdrive with some Linux thing, you can plug it in a computer and privately browse and nothing you do is stored on the computer's memory. It bounces your Internet traffic around like a game of three-card monte—"

"Half the nodes in the Internet misdirection network are run by US government agencies," Shapiro said.

"Is that how they tracked me?"

"Maybe. Keep talking."

"I didn't even do it from the shop. Or my apartment. I went to a coffee house."

Shapiro nodded, as if fog had burned away to reveal a mountain-top. "You took your phone with you?"

"Of course."

"That's probably how they tracked you. Your phone is always telling the network where it is."

Phillip's hands fell to the tabletop like dead birds. "How bad is it?"

"Like I said. Five years."

"Can you get me out of it?"

"If your father mortgages his house and borrows against the busi-ness, we might—might—get a not-guilty verdict from a jury trial."

Irving dropped his head into his hands. The tabletop jabbed at his elbows. Burn through all his money to try to save Phillip from his own foolishness? Of course he would.

Even if he would probably fail, even if he would have to beg for a charity bed at the Jewish nursing home, even if his son was a schlemiel who would find some other foolish mistake to make?

Of course he would.

Phillip spoke, voice small. "Is there another way?" His voice grew louder, faster. "I know, I could cooperate with the FBI, state's evidence."

"Can you give them anything they want and don't already have?"

"The websites where I posted—"

"They know the URL," Shapiro said. "Half the people posting there are undercover FBI agents."

"There must be something they want."

Irving lifted his head. "Surveillance video from the shop. The FBI can use it to identify your Muslim customers."

Phillip winced. "I turned off the cameras every day you were out."

Irving's fists bunched… then his hands dropped to the tabletop, inches from his son's. Security video missing from one day a week for months, and he'd never noticed? Who was the schlemiel now?

"Wouldn't work anyway," Shapiro said. "The FBI already has a warrant."

"They're ransacking the shop now?" Irving asked. Shapiro's raised eyebrow told him the answer. FBI agents marching in and out of the shop, in full view of everyone…. He swallowed a tiny amount of saliva flavored with the tablet.

Phillip reached forward and patted Irving's hand. "I'm sorry, dad."

"There must be something else we can try," Phillip said.

"The FBI warrant will give them access to your credit card records."

Phillip shook his head. "The Muslim customers always paid cash."

Shapiro lifted his chin. "The only evidence they can get is from inside your head. How's your memory for faces?"

"Really strong," Phillip said. Irving gave half a shrug and half a nod when Shapiro glanced his way.

Shapiro kept talking to Phillip. "Think of the most memorable customers you can. Detailed description of one is better than vague talk about a hundred. While you do that, I'll call Landry to offer a deal. Probation for full cooperation."

Phillip nodded.

Irving spoke. "We need FBI protection, too. You know how Muslims can get violent. If they put together that Phillip gave evidence against them—"

"I'll try," Shapiro said.

"You gotta do more than try."

"Is a try without a guarantee worse than five years in prison?" Shapiro said. "I'm going to call Landry now." He tapped the record button to off, then picked up his phone. A moment later he stepped into the hallway. Moments after that, his voice percolated through the gap between the door and the scuffed vinyl tile.

Irving sat with his eyes closed and his hands flat on the table. He couldn't blame Phillip, not fully. What had he done wrong when raising his son, to end up here?

"I hope Shapiro can get us a good deal," Phillip said.

"He's the best." In his own ears, his voice sounded like it came from a million miles away. He couldn't imagine what it sounded like to his son.

Phillip's soft hand slid over the veiny, bony back of Irving's. His voice sounded genuine. "Dad, I'm sorry."

Irving sloughed out a breath. Perhaps when raising his son, he'd done at least one thing right.

THE THIRTY-SECOND AMENDMENT

The Supreme Court shall consist of nine Judges, and all Judges of both the Supreme and inferior Courts, shall hold their Offices for a term of eighteen years.

The terms of the Judges of the Supreme Court shall be staggered, such that the term of one Judge shall end on the Thirty-first day of August of every odd-numbered Year.

The term of any Judge of either the Supreme or an inferior Court sitting as of the ratification of this amendment shall not be changed. For a Judge of the Supreme Court now sitting, his or her successor shall serve for the shortest possible term consistent with the first and second sections of this amendment.

The tall windows behind President Edward Slovachek looked out on the White House lawn and spilled warm spring light over his shoulders onto the polished mahogany top of the conference table. Large enough for cabinet meetings, now only the President sat at the table. The only sounds came from the tap of fingers on tablets, both his and those of his two aides seated along the windowed wall behind him; the faint buzz of the palm-sized Twenty-Eighth Amendment drones recording audio and video from their stations in the air around him; and the tick of the clock high on the wall to his left.

1:58. Two minutes.

The corners of President Slovachek's mouth lifted. Senate Minority Leader Chowdhury knew who held the trump card. Chowdhury would be on time.

A minute later, a bustle came from the hallway outside. Directly across the room from President Slovachek, the doorknob rattled. Behind him, tablets thumped on the cushions of unused seats. His aides prepared to stand.

The President held out his hands, palms-down. "Follow my lead," he said quietly, his voice rich and deep as the soil of Texas' Czech belt. He stayed in his seat while the door opened.

Another assistant, a buxom lady of middle years and twangy voice, said from the doorway, "Mr. President, the Minority Leader."

"Come on in, Mr. Chowdhury."

Chowdhury stepped past the assistant and across the threshold and another drone followed him. An inch over six feet—the Senate Minority Leader came from an Indian-American generation that decided US cows weren't sacred, but were instead a good source of protein—with lively brown eyes and a full head of wavy black hair. But a lot more gray salted the black, and purplish bags puffed under his eyes, than President Slovachek remembered from the last time they'd been in the same room.

After Chowdhury fully entered the room, President Slovachek slowly stood to his full height of six-three. An affable smile, a hand extended across the table. The courtesies emphasized his position of strength. He gripped Chowdhury's hand firmly, without the need to squeeze the other man's bones together or twist open his wrist.

He put a trace of Texas into his voice. "Good to see you again, Sunil. Take a seat. How are the grandkids?"

Chowdhury sat opposite the President. If the meeting wore deeper into the afternoon, the lowering sun would make him squint. "They're doing well, Mr. President. Jennifer got married two months ago...."

A couple of minutes of chit-chat ensued. Chowdhury's face turned more and more sour as the small talk went on. Eventually, President

Slovachek took him off the hook and got down to business. "The Supreme Court situation is a hell of a thing, isn't it?"

Chowdhury gave a brisk little nod. "We all knew the last two life appointees would leave the Court at some time."

"But not the same time." President Slovachek twisted the knife a little. "Especially not Crysta Kimbrough." In her forties when she joined the court, the last appointment before the Thirty-Second Amendment passed.

"Her death was tragic," Chowdhury said.

Lurid, more like—the murder in a murder-suicide perpetrated by her long-time companion—but a thousand social studies classes watched them live through the cameras of the circling drones, and ten thousand more would download the video tomorrow. It would be beneath the dignity of his office for President Slovachek to bring up the sordid details.

And Chowdhury was right, in a sense. Some tragic flaw of Kimbrough led her partner to bludgeon her to death in the kitchen of their Georgetown townhouse. "Sure was," the President said.

"Three appointees now. That's an awesome responsibility for you. And I don't think the drafters of the Thirty-Second ever contemplated a situation like this. Their whole point was to regularize the terms of the Justices to prevent drastic, generational shifts in the tone of the Court. To reduce partisan squabbling such as we saw over—" Chowdhury's fingers plucked the air for dusty names. "—Kavanaugh and—"

"How many of your candidates do you want me to nominate?"

Chowdhury blinked a single time. "Just one. Emerson Huang. Stanford undergraduate, a law degree from Harvard, he's a judge in the Southern District of Arizona. Well respected by judges, lawyers, law professors...."

"Why should I nominate him?" He gestured at one of the drones. "Put it on the record."

"As I was saying, the drafters of the Thirty-Second Amendment wanted to restore the Supreme Court to the level of bipartisanship the founding fathers intended. By nominating Huang, you'll show that same level of honor and respect for our country's ideals. The history books will speak highly of you long after we walk these halls for the last time."

A laugh broke through President Slovachek's grin. "The founding fathers? You know that Jefferson hated Hamilton? That Adams hated Jefferson?" He shook his head and laughed more. "You know all those ideals they talk about in social studies classes, separation of powers, checks and balances? The founding fathers put those in because they knew how bitter and factional they were to one another and assumed, rightly, that their successors would be the same."

Chowdhury hesitated, then said, "Because you're speaking in those terms, Mr. President, then I'll join you. If you nominate Huang, the Senate minority will work with you on a number of pieces of legislation. Funding the laser propulsion system for the interstellar probe is something we're not otherwise likely to vote for."

Mirth remained on President Slovachek's face, tempered now by a narrowing of his eyes. "You're desperate for the Court to declare unconstitutional the Bitcoin law."

"It's no secret I voted against it. Leading economists made it clear the gold standard led to the Great Depression. A Bitcoin standard would create the same deflationary spiral and the same—yes, Mr. President, I know you have other leading economists who claim the Great Depression was caused by the bursting of a technological innovation bubble, or mismanagement by the Federal Reserve Bank—"

President Slovachek laughed. "It's just you, me, and the American people here, Sunny. So we're going to shoot straight. You don't care whether the Bitcoin standard is constitutional or not. Some big boys in the shadows will lose billions if we replace their fiat dollars with ones denominated by Bitcoin and you're doing their bidding."

Chowdhury paled a moment, then knitted his eyebrows and plunged ahead. "The American people have seen my every public move for decades. They know I've never taken orders from any 'big boys in the shadows,' so don't slander me."

"Did I say you took orders?" President Slovachek drew out the next word. "No. But we know those billionaires are in the shadows, and we know they make their wishes known to people who know people you know. Your aides, your friends and family here and back in Kentucky. Through those channels, you can act on the wishes of the billionaires and still look clean."

Chowdhury clamped his lips together. Pinned anger darted around his brown eyes. "There are big boys in your shadows too, Mr. President. Holders of Bitcoin will earn a thousand percent profit overnight and they made sure you knew it, didn't they?"

The President gave Chowdhury a serious look, chased by a wry smile that flickered over his mouth. He turned to the afternoon glow coming through the windows. Six months into his second term. Did that make him a lame duck, or one with nothing to lose?

"There's one thing about policy making, Sunny, they don't teach the kids in social studies class."

Voice wary, Chowdhury asked, "What's that?"

"There's next to nothing to do with high principles and what's good for all Americans. It's almost all about one special interest trying to wring a buck out of another. Or, worse, both agreeing to split among themselves two bucks they wring out of the taxpayer. Sure, your party dresses up the money-grabbing with one set of vaguely stirring words, while my party uses another set. But between you and me, we know that hardly matters."

Chowdhury peered at the President, then sniffed out a chuckle. He angled his head at a drone. "Are you telling the American people that there's no difference between fiat dollars and a Bitcoin standard?"

"No. There's plenty of difference. Because your special interest is a handful of billionaires. My special interest is two hundred million productive Americans." President Slovachek grinned.

Chowdhury calmed himself over a couple of breaths. "You won't nominate Huang."

"Nope."

"You won't get your interstellar probe."

"Maybe not. I'd very much like it, but I can live without it." President Slovachek shrugged. "The stars will be there for my successor."

ABOUT THE AUTHOR

Raymund Eich files patent applications, earned a Ph.D., won a national quiz bowl championship, writes science fiction and fantasy, and affirms Robert Heinlein's dictum that specialization is for insects. In a typical day, he may talk with biochemists, electrical engineers, patent attorneys, epileptologists, and rocket scientists. Hundreds of papers cite his graduate research on the reactions of nitric oxide with heme proteins.

Connect with the author at **www.raymundeich.com** or scan the QR code below.

Sign up for his mailing list to receive exclusive, pre-release content about his upcoming books. Your email address will never be shared and you can unsubscribe at any time. Go to **www.raymundeich.com/mailing-list** or scan the QR code below.

Other Books by the Author

Stone Chalmers

Earth barely survived the 21st Century. Biotechnological and nuclear terrorism, civil war, famine, and ethnic cleansing killed billions. Thousands fled on warpdrive ships to colonize planets around distant suns.

In the 22nd century, after the United Nations established control over Earth, it opened wormhole links to the distant colonies, to prevent a repeat of the previous century's chaos on a galactic scale.

Enter operative Stone Chalmers. Spy. Assassin. Instrument maintaining the UN's order on the settled galaxy.

Opposing him are hostile forces on colony worlds… and within the UN itself.

When Stone clashes with those forces, the UN—and every human world—will be transformed forever.

Learn more about the Stone Chalmers series at **www.cv2books.com/stone-chalmers**, or scan the QR code below.

The Progress of Mankind (#1)

To maintain order in the 22nd century, the UN relocates undesirables through artificial wormholes onto colony planets. Everyone benefits… except the planets' original colonists.

Now, the newly rediscovered colony of New Moravia learns the UN's plan and fights back.

The Greater Glory of God (#2)

Thousands fled the chaos of the 21st century on rogue warpdrive ships to settle colony planets. When Earth reunified in the 22nd, its fleets rediscovered the colonies and hunted down the warpdrive ships.

Every warpdrive ship but one.

To All High Emprise Consecrated (#3)

After unifying Earth, the UN has rediscovered the colony of Minerva. Prosperous and technologically advanced, Minerva quickly submits to UN supremacy.

Surprisingly quickly…

In Public Convocation Assembled (#4)

After unifying Earth, the UN controls all human colonies scattered through the galaxy by means of wormholes, warpdrive ships, and ruthless operatives. Operatives working to strengthen the UN.

Or destroy it.

The Confederated Worlds

The purpose of all other combat arms is to put the infantryman in sole possession of the battlefield.

A thousand years from now, while Earth sleeps in virtual reality, three polities—the Confederated Worlds, the Unity, and the Progressive Republic—strive to connect the scattered, terraformed worlds of humankind by artificial wormholes. When they meet, they clash, in a decades-long struggle of arms that will embroil every human world, in which dedication to duty liberates worlds—and oneself.

Learn more about the Confederated Worlds series at **www.cv2books.com/the-confederated-worlds**, or scan the QR code below.

Take the Shilling (Book 1)

The Confederated Worlds implanted in his brain the skills to make him a soldier. Tomas Neumann had to learn for himself how to survive interstellar war.

Operation Iago (Book 2)

The Confederated Worlds lost the war. Can Lt. Tomas Neumann win the peace against elusive, deceptive foes out to turn the Confederated Worlds against itself?

A Bodyguard of Lies (Book 3)

Assigned to the halls of power, only Capt. Tomas Neumann can save the Confederated Worlds from the ultimate treachery.

Novels

The Blank Slate

Neuroscience entrepreneur Clay Shieffer must stop a tyrannical president… because he unwittingly gave the tyrant power over the human mind.

New California

After New California's founder committed suicide, two men vied to rule the colony.

Ashwin George, supported by the colony's elite and the Chinese company dominating half the settled galaxy.

Against him, Desmond Park, nanotechnology engineer, armed with the most formidable weapon of all.

A single idea.

The Reincarnation Run

Solitary spacejock Landry Krieger smuggled people past the watchful eyes of interstellar governments, in hiding spaces he built in his ship, *Midnight Angel*.

When the priests of Tao Pacem sought his services, he resisted. Brown robes? Yin-yang symbols? Dreams of sparking a rebelling by sneaking the reincarnation of their spiritual leader to their oppressed homeworld? After Landry's earlier experiences with religious leaders, he needed more reason than money to say *yes*.

He got that reason, when an arrogant agent of the oppressors tried to scare him off the job.

Short Novels

The ALECS Quartet

He had a month to learn the planet's mysteries—and Juliette's.

His cover story: return to Elard to dismantle his sect's missionary work to the planet's natives.

His true mission: investigate decades-old mysteries of love and death.

His objective: return to Earth with his discovery.

If he can.

A Mighty Fortress

Theodore and his team from the Lutheran Interstellar Terraforming Society would transform a barren, rocky world into a refuge of faith and life.

Or die trying.

Collections

The First Voyages: The Complete Science Fiction Stories 1998-2012

From 21st century asteroid settlements to World War II Romania, from an Earth dominated by immortal aliens to Christ's empty tomb, a fresh, distinctive voice in science fiction will take you on journeys to the photosphere of the sun, the coding regions of DNA, and the complexities of the human psyche.

Stage Separations: The Complete Science Fiction Stories 2013-2018

In these pages, you can...

...race against time to solve mysteries hidden in a planet's vast desert—and in a woman's heart ...learn the true story of a president's assassination ...journey 14,000 miles to a high-tech fountain of youth ...win or go "home"—to an Earth you've never seen

and explore six other worlds created by a distinctive voice in twenty-first century science fiction.